BOOK ANALYSIS

By Tara Dorrell

Schindler's Ark

BY THOMAS KENEALLY

THOMAS KENEALLY

AUSTRALIAN NOVELIST AND PLAYWRIGHT

- **Born in Sydney in 1935.**
- **Notable works:**
  - *Searching for Schindler* (2007), memoir
  - *The Daughters of Mars* (2012), novel
  - *Crimes of the Father* (2016), novel

The Australian novelist Thomas Keneally is best known for the novel *Schindler's Ark*, later adapted into the critically acclaimed film *Schindler's List*. Although he initially trained for a Catholic priesthood at St Patrick's Seminary, Manly, Keneally later left without being ordained, and instead worked as a schoolteacher, before eventually becoming a novelist and lecturer at the University of New England.

Many of his works use historical material as their basis, and he has shown an interest in moral dilemmas, as well as the conflict between an individual and authority. His writing has been described as leaning towards melodrama, but nonetheless holds a place in both the Australian and international mainstream. Through *Schindler's Ark,* he shone a light on the bravest people in Europe's darkest moment, and in doing so encouraged people to remember both those who suffered in the Holocaust and those who did what they could to lessen the suffering.

SCHINDLER'S ARK

THE WORST OF MANKIND AND THE BEST OF HUMANITY

- **Genre:** novel
- **Reference edition:** Keneally, T. (2007) *Schindler's Ark.* London: Serpentine Publishing.
- **1st edition:** 1982
- **Themes:** World War II, Holocaust, denial, dehumanisation, power, defiance

Schindler's Ark is based on the true story of Oskar Schindler, a German businessman who saved over a thousand Jews from concentration camps like Auschwitz during World War II. Thomas Keneally was only prompted to write the novel after being convinced by a salesman in Beverly Hills, LA – who was in fact one of the Jews saved by Schindler, Leopold Pfefferberg, mentioned in the book. Although very readable, the novel does not hide the brutality of history, and has been cited as restoring faith in humanity. By recounting the well-known events of the war though personal eye-witness accounts and retellings, it gives attention to the individuals affected by the war whose voices would not be heard otherwise. In 1982, *Schindler's Ark* won the Man Booker Prize for Fiction, and the novel was later adapted by Steven Spielberg into the award-winning film *Schindler's List.*

SUMMARY

THE BEGINNING OF A NIGHTMARE

Keneally traces the true events of Oskar Schindler's work in World War II through the course of the novel, starting with Schindler's own roots as a Sudetenland German; young, ambitious and in love, uncaring of "race, blood and soil" (p. 38) and unaware of how crucial a role these things would play in his life. Alongside Keneally's account of Schindler, the novel also intermittently focuses on other eye-witness accounts and retellings – some key to the plot, others not – of those who suffered the horrors of the ghettos, concentration camps and everything that led up to them. Glimpses of Helen Hirsch and Leopold "Poldek" Pfefferberg, among others, are scattered throughout, and the voices and names of those who perish are as important as any who survive.

A self-made man and business entrepreneur, Oskar Schindler sets about establishing a factory in Nazi-occupied Cracow, using generous bribes of jewels, coffee and alcohol, as well as his own gift with people, to effectively create a safe haven for the increasingly persecuted Jewish population. Along with Itzhak Stern, Schindler's source of local information, and Victoria Klonowska, his hard-headed Polish secretary, Schindler creates work in Deutsche Emailwaren Fabrik, his enamels factory, citing his Jewish employees as valuable workers vital to the war effort. In doing so, he simultaneously provides work and saves them from excessive harm or death at the hands of the SS. As Schindler's factory comes into being, life for the Jews in Cracow becomes steadily worse. They are slowly moved into a ghetto on the outskirts of the city, the conditions of which are cramped and unquestionably terrible, but at the same time inspire nostalgia for the "old ghetto of Kazimierz" (p. 94). This ghetto, however, is under the control of the Ordnungdienst (OD), the Jewish Ghetto Police, who are vicious to their own people in the hopes of saving their individual families. At the same time that the OD gain control of the ghetto, Schindler finds himself arrested twice, once having been betrayed, and the second time for kissing a Jewish girl in a moment of gaiety on his birthday. Both times he manages to avoid detainment for more than a few days, thanks to his numerous contacts among high-ranking Nazi officials, and the intelligence of his secretary and lover, Klonowska.

INTO THE CAMPS

Schindler himself becomes aware of the cruelty of the ghettos when one afternoon he and another girlfriend, Ingrid, ride horses across the hills overlooking the Jewish quarter. A new requirement for a *Blauschein* (or blue sticker) in order to work saw half the population of the ghetto being forcibly taken into the newly forming work camps, or else shot for resisting. It is here that Oskar sees a mother and son killed in cold blood for trying to hide from the SS, all in plain view of a toddler in a red coat who only manages to escape by luck. Rumours of the abhorrent conditions of the camps begin to circulate, and Schindler is called down to Budapest by Turkish Zionists who are concerned about the treatment of their fellow Jews. Schindler's account of the treatment of Jews in the ghettos and the even more disgusting treatment of them in the camps is juxtaposed with the end of the ghetto in Cracow itself, which is finally replaced with Plaszów – the city's very own concentration camp.

With the camp comes the arrival of Commandant Amon Goeth, a brutal and temperamental man with a genuine love for killing. He is thoroughly despised by Schindler, although the latter maintains a pretence of congeniality in order to stay in his favour and thus save as many Jewish prisoners as possible. Goeth takes pleasure in killing his Jewish prisoners as he pleases, and Schindler quickly concludes that the best possible solution for his workers is to create a sub-camp of his own, distanced from the whims of the Commandant and with more food and water than any other camp in Nazi-occupied Poland. Competition to get into his camp is fierce, and many prisoners plead and offer bribes for the safety of themselves or their family. Although Schindler manages to bring the majority of his workers into his sub-camp, a few families and individuals remain at Plaszów, where the chances of death rapidly increase for them.

WHOEVER SAVES ONE LIFE SAVES THE WORLD ENTIRE

The prospect of Russian victory on the Eastern Front begins to grow more certain, and as it does the inmates of Plaszów begin to be shipped off to Auschwitz, the closing of the camp now imminent. Faced with the high chance of losing all the Jewish workers he has so far managed to keep safe, Schindler manages to convince Goeth to let him build an entirely new camp, Brinnlitz, where his skilled workers could supposedly continue to work for him. Although it comes at enormous expense, Schindler manages, and together with Itzhak Stern, compiles the list which will eventually save thousands of people from Auschwitz.

Although the trains bringing the women and children to Brinnlitz are initially redirected to Auschwitz, Schindler and his wife Emilie are eventually able to bring them to safety. In the midst of this, Schindler himself is once more arrested, this time for his connections with Goeth, who has now also been imprisoned. The Jewish workers spend the remainder of the war in Brinnlitz, fighting illnesses like typhus but in far better conditions than anything a genuine Nazi camp would have provided. A surprise inspection of the factory results in the few children present and their fathers, being taken to Auschwitz, but the promise of an end to the war means they manage to survive, getting stamped as workers rather than being sent straight to the gas chambers. As the factory is entirely a pretence and produces nothing of use, Schindler runs out of money in 1945; his future is left unclear as a Nazi Party member in a country now under the control of the Allies. Before leaving, his workers present him with a letter in Hebrew and an engraved ring bearing the words "Whoever saves one life saves the world entire" (p. 399).

The epilogue reveals how Schindler and his wife leave for Buenos Aires, as they are no longer safe in Germany as former members of the Nazi Party. However, Schindler eventually abandons Emilie to return to Germany, and attempts to re-establish his life as a businessman there. Most of his survivors leave Germany entirely, many (including Stern) going to Jerusalem, where they lobby Western governments for a pension for Oskar given his work in the war. Schindler himself dies in 1974 and is buried – as per his wishes – in Jerusalem.

CHARACTER STUDY

OSKAR SCHINDLER

Described as a blond-haired, blue-eyed, tall young man, Oskar Schindler is from the start an ambitious businessman with a head for enterprise. Although the novel follows his personal mission to save as many Jews as possible from the gas chambers in the concentration camps, Keneally takes care to note that he is not a wholly virtuous and innocent man. While he is prone to womanising and initially works with the intent of becoming more successful than his father, over the course of the novel Schindler does become a saviour of sorts to the people of the Plaszów camp in Cracow. He repeatedly promises he is "going to get you *all* out" (p. 277), with an authority that appears almost divine – if Schindler promises it, it must be so.

Schindler's Ark is as much a story about a very ordinary man with a crisis of conscience at a time when it matters most as a story about survival against the worst of odds. Oskar Schindler is never the idealised war hero one might expect: Keneally makes it clear that it is not his deeply-rooted sense of right and wrong that carries him through the war, but rather his charm, gusto, and skills as a con-man that enable him to repeatedly outwit the SS. He joins the Nazi Party for the business it will bring him and is seemingly indifferent to the displacement of the Jews whose apartment he is given. It is only because of the prologue, which depicts the man Schindler becomes, obsessed with saving as many Jews as possible, that the reader can believe the ambitious man at the start of the novel will do any good at all. Over time, and as the result of a few key encounters and events, Schindler changes from a man indifferent to the horrors around him to one filled with compassion for the people he takes as his own. His wife later stated that Schindler had "done nothing astounding before the war and nothing exceptional since" (p. 428) – it is fortunate, then, that his particular skill set was needed more than ever in the early days of the conflict.

AMON GOETH

Upon Goeth's initial introduction, Keneally emphasises how he and Schindler are physically similar: they are both large, heavily built men, and are both incredibly intimidating. The similarities do not stop there, however: both men have an affinity for drink and both are enthusiastic about life's sexual pleasures. Despite this, Goeth is the classical antithesis to Schindler, both arguably holding the potential to become the other, but a difference in moral stances leading them to work against one another. Goeth comes across as highly temperamental: the entire Plaszów camp is run on his whims and fancies. He is described as having often shot someone "who was passing" (p. 31) for his leisure, yet Pfefferberg manages to escape death because the Commandant was amused by him. With a love for music, particularly the Rosner Brothers' playing, and for the finer things in life, Goeth's word is law in the camp, and Schindler has to take care to remain in his good books in order to protect his workers. He somehow manages to keep Goeth convinced they are close friends, when in reality he despises him.

Goeth is eventually imprisoned: he later reappears at the Brinnlitz camp, and while the prisoners there are still mostly terrified of him, it is clear his power is nearly all gone – he now has to complain to Schindler that the Jewish workers do not respect him. He is a demonstration of the utter inhumanity that could be found during the war – historically significant in that he *exists*, proof that, while the war created heroes like Schindler, it also created monsters like Goeth.

ITZHAK STERN

Itzhak Stern accompanies Schindler from the beginning of the novel until the end, and is his connection to the Jewish people he is trying to save and his voice of reason throughout. He is essentially the brains behind Schindler's enterprise, although he is originally contemptuous of Schindler's gruff attempts at solidarity when Stern is required by law to state that he is a Jew. While he is made to work for Schindler, Stern turns it into an opportunity to help as many of his people as he can, simultaneously becoming a genuine friend and confidant to Schindler towards the end. It is he who presents Schindler with the ring the Jews created, inscribed with a verse from the Talmud – "He who saves a single life saves the world entire" (p. 399). Stern had quoted these very lines at the start of the novel, foreshadowing the events that follow and potentially planting the seed needed for Schindler to save as many people as possible.

EMILIE SCHINDLER

Emilie Schindler is Oskar's long-suffering wife, who later aids him in feeding and caring for the workers at Brinnlitz. The couple marry after just a few weeks of courtship, when Oskar is young and in love and Emilie is naïve and eager to leave her stagnant hometown. Said to be "nunlike, gracious, unsophisticated" (p. 40), Emilie nevertheless grows to become a "figure of quiet dignity" (p. 428), and was one of Keneally's sources in writing the book. Despite this, for much of the novel she is absent. She lives away from her husband's factory in Cracow, and also away from his relationships with a multitude of women, all of whom are equally aware of one another.

Upon the creation of Brinnlitz, Emilie returns to live with Schindler, and becomes a steady presence within the new camp, nursing feverish Jews back to health and bringing them food with quiet and enduring patience. Following the end of the war, she escapes to Buenos Aires with her husband, living there alone when he abandons her to return to Germany. She symbolises all the women whose voices and efforts were lost in the war, but who were just as vital to the survival of thousands, although rarely acknowledged.

ANALYSIS

BASED ON REAL EVENTS

Although the book is written in the form of a novel, Keneally uses eyewitness accounts to tell the story. In the author's note that prefaces the text, he describes how he was approached in Beverly Hills, Los Angeles, by none other than Leopold Pfefferberg, a Jew saved by Schindler who appears numerous times throughout the book. In addition to Pferfferberg's recollections, Keneally relied on testimonies of and interviews with at least 50 survivors from Schindler's factory, as well as the letters and documents of Oskar Schindler's wartime associates and friends. The resulting book created by Keneally and these witnesses is an account that reads half like a novel, half like a history textbook. It is filled with the horrifying statistics of the war – 13 000 women prisoners at Plaszów, 1200 people forced into six barracks – but lacks the cold indifference typically found in history books. Keneally's skill as a writer transforms lives of violence, fear, and submission into something readable, without losing the voices of those affected in the process.

The Holocaust was one of the most horrific events in World War II, and involved the systematic genocide of around six million European Jews. Given that this is a difficult subject to approach but one that can never be forgotten, Keneally's book reminded the world of the trauma of the event, and encouraged people not to become complacent in remembering it. He intertwines Schindler's actions with the lives of the people he helps, providing snapshots of children, Rabbis and servants, and in doing so brings to light the stories of people who would have become just another number, lost in the brutality of the concentration camps and the rush of the aftermath.

THE ROLE OF WOMEN

In the story of Schindler and his Moses-like crusade to save the Jews of Plaszów camp, the women in the text are often lost. Keneally acknowledges early on that Schindler himself was a womaniser: he always seems to be involved with at least three women, one of whom is his wife. Schindler's own actions towards women are often seen as pardonable, as his lovers never make a complaint, and his behaviour appears insignificant compared with the Holocaust. However, this simply highlights the extended torment, sexual as well as violent, that plagues the women in *Schindler's Ark*, and indeed in Nazi-occupied Europe itself. Although it is often written off as not as traumatic as what took place in the concentration camps, the victimisation of women during the war was another part of the brutality against them, and should not be made light of. As the hero of the text is a womaniser, the harm done to women as a result of their gender is downplayed: the cruelty faced by women such as Helen Hirsch at the hands of the SS officers is viewed as simply an unavoidable part of the war, rather than an additional atrocity.

Despite this, the women in the novel never fail to act with dignity, and although they are often ignored, they are of just as much value to Schindler's efforts and the fight for humanity and survival as the men. Oskar Schindler was arrested three times over the course of the war, and twice before his haven was even set up. It was always Schindler's pretty, hard-headed secretary Victoria Klonowska who managed to get him released, as she always knew exactly the right people to call and the right words to say. Similarly, Schindler's own wife, Emilie, proves to be a necessary and stabilising presence in Brinnlitz, although she too becomes overshadowed by the "Oskar legend" (p. 361), just as countless women throughout history become subsumed by their male counterparts.

Time and again the women are shown to be just as resilient as the men. One example of this is the last remaining nurse in the Cracow ghetto before it is shut down. Only four patients who cannot be moved, two doctors and the nurse are left, and the doctors are certain in the knowledge that none of them will survive. As the kindest thing to do is to euthanise the prisoners before the Nazis get to them, the nurse is asked to administer a lethal dose of cyanide to each patient, while the doctors do the same to each other. Although we never find out whether or not the nurse also commits suicide, the words of one doctor, "The woman is the hero of this" (p. 197), are a reminder of the bravery women displayed during the Holocaust. Their persistence and determination are also emphasised: Regina Perlman-Rodriguez does everything she can to convince Schindler to let her parents into his camp, knowing of his womanising tendencies and using them to her advantage. Similarly, a young emissary is sent to Commandant Goeth voluntarily, and "deal[s] courageously" (p.346) with whatever she faces there – Keneally is unclear on whether her task involves sexual favours, but it is clear that it is dangerous and unenviable regardless.

Although she is not a woman, the little girl in red, Genia, signals a moment of epiphany for Schindler, when he watches her evade the SS soldiers killing Jews in the street by pure luck. Her childish innocence is juxtaposed with shocking and graphic deaths, and she comes to symbolise the innocence and youth lost as a result of the war. While Schindler never finds out if she survives, her escape does become a turning point for him, the moment where he truly decides that he has to get these people out, beyond potentially making a profit.

In addition to these individual episodes, the fact

that the female survivors of Plaszów still end up suffering through Auschwitz in addition to all their previous trauma just goes to highlight their own strength and will to live, so often overshadowed by the actions of the men around them. It is arguably insensitive to make metaphors of real-life people and events, yet the determination to persevere through life is aptly symbolised in the women of the text, the traditional bearers of life.

BECOMING *SCHINDLER'S LIST*

Following book's success as an award-winning international bestseller, Leopold Pfefferberg turned his sights to the silver screen, seeking someone who could transform it into a film or TV show in order to further people's awareness of Oskar Schindler and his actions. Steven Spielberg, at the time already known for films like *Jaws* (1975) and his *Indiana Jones* series, was sent a *New York Times* review of the novel, and was encouraged to take on the project. Spielberg was initially hesitant, uncertain of whether he was a mature enough filmmaker for such sombre subject matter. The film would also touch on deeply personal subject matter: Spielberg himself came from an Orthodox Jewish family. Regardless, he did eventually become the director, and *Schindler's List*, starring Liam Neeson (British actor, born in 1952), Ralph Fiennes (English actor, born in 1962) and Ben Kingsley (English actor, born in 1943) was released in 1993.

Although Thomas Keneally was originally asked to write the script for the film, he failed to adequately condense the story, and the final draft was instead written by Steven Zaillian (American screenwriter, born in 1953). A significant portion of the film focuses on the liquidation of the Cracow ghetto, an intensely unforgettable episode for the audience. Spielberg's adaptation also maintained some of the same imagery found in Keneally's book, namely the symbolism of the little girl Genia in her red coat, the only use of colour in an otherwise black and white film.

Schindler's List was a highly successful film, achieving immense critical acclaim and the support of the popular press, as well as world leaders. There was a modicum of controversy surrounding it, as some critics felt the Holocaust to be too serious a subject for cinematic viewing, which could potentially brush over or downplay the true horror of the event. Spielberg was aware of this possibility when filming, and thus directed a film that views more like a documentary than anything made purely for entertainment, just as *Schindler's Ark* straddles the line between being a historical retelling and a novel.

FURTHER REFLECTION

SOME QUESTIONS TO THINK ABOUT...

- Compare the characters of Amon Goeth and Oskar Schindler. In what ways are they similar and different?
- Do you think Keneally made the right decision to write *Schindler's Ark* in the form of a novel? Why/why not?
- As this is an account of real people during wartime, do you think their actions can be judged the same way you might judge a fictional character? Explain your answer.
- Emilie Schindler said "Oskar had done nothing astounding before the war and nothing exceptional since" (p. 428). How do you think war changes people's characters – and do you think that change is permanent?
- How do you think the book compares to the well-known adaption, *Schindler's List*?
- Explore the theme of moral ambiguity in *Schindler's Ark*.

- What do you think a 21st-century reader can stand to learn from the book?
- Keneally scatter the accounts of a multitude of characters throughout the novel – do you think this is effective in creating a well-rounded portrayal of the Holocaust?
- How do romantic relationships figure in the text? Is there room for them during a war?

We want to hear from you!
Leave a comment on your online library
and share your favourite books on social media!

FURTHER READING

REFERENCE EDITION

- Keneally, T. (2007) *Schindler's Ark.* London: Serpentine Publishing.

REFERENCE STUDIES

- Bee, A. (2013) Schindler's Ark by Thomas Keneally – review. *The Guardian.* [Online]. [Accessed 12 January 2019]. Available from: <https://www.theguardian.com/childrens-books-site/2013/sep/25/review-schindler-s-ark-by-thomas-keneally>

- Ebert, R. (2002) In Praise of Love. *RogerEbert.com.* [Online]. [Accessed 12 January 2019]. Available from: <https://www.rogerebert.com/reviews/in-praise-of-love-2002>

- McBride, J. (2011) *Steven Spielberg: A Biography.* New York: Simon and Schuster.

- Ryan, S. (No date) Thomas Keneally. *Australian Catholic University.* [Online]. [Accessed 12 January 2019]. Available from: <https://resource.acu.edu.au/siryan/Academy/author%20pages/keneally,%20thomas.htm>

ADDITIONAL SOURCES

- Crowe, D. (2004) *Oskar Schindler: The Untold Account of His Life, Wartime Activities, and the True Story Behind the List.* Colorado: Westview Press.

- Keneally, T. (2007) *Searching for Schindler: A Memoir.* London: Hodder Publishing

ADAPTATIONS

- *Schindler's List.* (1993) [Film]. Steven Spielberg Dir. USA: Amblin Entertainment.

www.brightsummaries.com

Ebook EAN: 9782808017008

Paperback EAN: 9782808017015

Legal Deposit: D/2019/12603/17

Cover: © Primento

Digital conception by Primento, the digital partner of
publishers.